IN A TIME OF DISTANCE

IN A TIME OF DISTANCE

and Other Poems

ALEXANDER McCALL SMITH

with illustrations by
IAIN McINTOSH

Pantheon Books

New York

Copyright © 2020, 2021 by Alexander McCall Smith
Illustrations copyright © 2020 by Iain McIntosh

All rights reserved. Published in the United States by Pantheon
Books, a division of Penguin Random House LLC, New York.
Originally published in hardcover in Great Britain by Polygon
Books, an imprint of Birlinn Limited, Edinburgh, in 2020.

Pantheon Books and colophon are registered
trademarks of Penguin Random House LLC.

Library of Congress Cataloging-in-Publication Data
Names: McCall Smith, Alexander, [date] author. |
McIntosh, Iain, illustrator.
Title: In a time of distance : and other poems /
Alexander McCall Smith ; illustrated by Iain McIntosh.
Description: First American edition. New York : Pantheon Books, 2022
Identifiers: LCCN 2021026982 (print) | LCCN 2021026983 (ebook) |
ISBN 9780593315989 (hardcover) | ISBN 9780593315996 (ebook)
Subjects: LCSH: McCall Smith, Alexander, [date]—
Travel—Poetry. | LCGFT: Poetry.
Classification: LCC PR6063.C326 I5 2022 (print) |
LCC PR6063.C326 (ebook) | DDC 821/.914—dc23
LC record available at https://lccn.loc.gov/2021026982
LC ebook record available at https://lccn.loc.gov/2021026983

www.pantheonbooks.com

Jacket images by Iain McIntosh
Jacket design by Abigail Salvesen

Printed in the United States of America
First United States Edition
2 4 6 8 9 7 5 3 1

CONTENTS

UNRELATED POEMS

A number of these poems were, on their creation, dedicated to particular people. Sometimes the dedicatees happened to be there at the time of writing; on other occasions the poem seemed just right for them.

These poems are:

"A Typology of Angels," *for Iain McIntosh*
"Holy River," *for Prince Richard Holkar*
"Feel Glorious," *for Hugh Raven*
"Do Not Lean Again," *for Neil and Judy Swan*
"Giraffe, Zebra," *for Richard Neville-Towle and Caroline Hahn*
"On Looking at a Child," *for Ivy Rose Mant*
"The Goodness of Books," *for Laura Bush*
"Graham Greene," *for Joseph Kanon*
"A Maker of Beautiful Books," *for Stephanie Wolfe Murray*
"Goodbye to the Ionian," *for Nicky Wood*
"St. Kilda," *for Fergus Hall*
"Fish, and the Thoughts of Fish," *for Douglas Mant*
"Saving an Oak Tree," *for Malcolm Wood*

In a Time of Distance

A poem, in the mind of its creator, is often closely associated with the memory of a place, or of a time, or of something momentarily glimpsed and then seared into memory. Here is a poem that comes from a scene I saw many years ago in the Western Highlands of Scotland. I was travelling on a remote road and suddenly noticed that hung out on the washing line outside a white-painted croft house, alongside the ordinary items one sees on a washing line—shirts and so on—was a man's suit. The nearest dry cleaner must have been hours away, and so I should not have been surprised to see a suit being washed. But I was, and the image has remained with me over the intervening decades. It was a bright day, and the sun was upon the green of the fields and the blue of the sea. A stiff wind blew against the washing pegged out to dry, animating it in a strange choreography. I realised at the time that this was something I would remember for a long time—and that is what I have done. If I close my eyes, I see it. And I smell the breeze from the sea, which is pristine in those parts, and I feel regret for what has gone, as we all must do when we think back to times when the world was fresh to us.

A WASHING LINE OUTSIDE A CROFT HOUSE

Here on a line outside a croft
A suit has been hung,
A dark suit, old-fashioned,
The wear of some older man
For the regulated Sunday
Of a Highland kirk; its arms,
Filled with wind, beat time,
Remind us of half-remembered rhythms;

Remind us of the line of green between the sea
And the land behind the sea, that strip of flowers
And of whitened shells they call machair;

Remind us of that beat of the heart
That is this land, the unexpected vision,
The simple facts of being.

A memory rarely stands by itself. There is the memory, and then there are the associations that it triggers. In this poem, an olfactory memory reminds me of a particular part of Scotland and of a time, a matter of a couple of weeks, I spent there—again a long time ago. But any discussion of memory may itself remind us of Proust, whose theories of memory are, remarkably, being proven by contemporary neuroscience. In this poem, the image of machair appears again. It haunts me in its beauty. It is the landscape that I would expect to find in heaven, if heaven were ever to exist. Forget the fountains and clouds of other notions of heaven—make it Scottish machair, with the sound of the waves breaking on the shore and the cry of seabirds on the wind.

TASTE AND MEMORY

For Proust it was the madeleine cake
Dipped into tea; an unexpected key
To a flood of memories; for any of us
A taste, a smell, may evoke moments
We had not dwelt on very much
But that were always there, half hidden
In the lumber room of our minds,
Reproachful of our forgetfulness
But generous in their rewards,
Restoring place and emotion,
Love, friendship, the small exchanges
That go with being who we are

And where, and in what ways,
We have lived our ordinary lives,
Reassuring us that we have not
Lost what we thought we had.

For me it is the smell of gorse,
The flowers of which briefly in summer
Are redolent of coconut; small patches
Of yellow in the dark green foliage,
They scent the air, cling to the breeze,
Surprise the walkers or the lovers,
Make them stop, interrogate
The evening air, then put away
That unexpected memory of coconut
Amidst memories of islands
And quiet glens, the secret places
Of this country on the edge of
A continent, an afterthought of land.

On a Hebridean island in my twentieth year
I passed a place where gorse had colonised
A fold of land near a stretch of machair—
The lovely name by which some shores
Are known—grass and broken shells
And tiny flowers, close to the green sea;
But it is the gorse that I remember,

And its floral smell, touched with notes
Of seaweed, of sea salt, of iodine,
Those things that one can smell—and taste—
On the breath of the Scottish islands.

I was happy then and wished
Those around me, and one friend in particular,
The happiness I felt; now it is gorse
That reminds me of that time,
Not noisily, or with insistence,
But quietly, discreetly, as the wind
May whisper gently in our ear.

One friend in particular: anybody may do for that. All that we need is somebody on whom we can focus our feelings of *gratitude*. The real test of love, or friendship, is whether we are *grateful* that the other exists. Auden captured that in his lines about how love requires an object, but almost anything will do—even, in his case, when he was a boy, a pumping engine that was "every bit as beautiful as you."

Here is another poem that will, I feel, always be closely associated in my mind with a very particular moment when people were required to live in conditions of isolation. This poem refers to that experience.

IN A TIME OF DISTANCE

The unexpected always happens in the way
The unexpected has always occurred:
While we are doing something else,
While we are thinking of altogether
Different things—matters that events
Then show to be every bit as unimportant
As our human concerns so often are;
And then, with the unexpected upon us,
We look at one another with a sort of surprise;
How could things possibly turn out this way
When we are so competent, so pleased
With the elaborate systems we've created—
Networks and satellites, intelligent machines,
Pills for every eventuality—except this one?

And so we turn again to face one another
And discover those things
We had almost forgotten,
But that, mercifully, are still there:
Love and friendship, not just for those
To whom we are closest, but also for those
Whom we do not know and of whom

Perhaps we have in the past been frightened;
The words *brother* and *sister*, powerful still,
Are brought out, dusted down,
Found to be still capable of expressing
What we feel for others, that precise concern;
Joined together in adversity
We discover things we had put aside:
Old board games with obscure rules,
Books we had been meaning to read,
Letters we had intended to write,
Things we had thought we might say
But for which we never found the time;
And from these discoveries of self, of time,
There comes a new realisation
That we have been in too much of a hurry,
That we have misused our fragile world,
That we have forgotten the claims of others
Who have been left behind;
We find that out in our seclusion,
In our silence; we commit ourselves afresh,
We look for a few bars of a song
That we used to sing together,
A long time ago; we give what we can,
We wait, knowing that when this is over
A lot of us—not all perhaps—but most,
Will be slightly different people,
And our world, though diminished,
Will be much bigger, its beauty revealed afresh.

Journeys

Script-writers like to talk about the journey that each character has. We must see that, they say. We must witness the development of character over time. People should not be the same at the beginning of a play or film as they are at the end; stability of character does not make for good entertainment.

So, a journey may be real or metaphorical. The real journey—one that involves ordinary transport across identifiable terrain—may be as rich in association, may give food for thought, just as much as any metaphorical journey.

Here is a journey into the land that lies to the south of Edinburgh—through the Scottish Borders.

OUR JOURNEYS

Driving one day into the Borders,
That quiet landscape where so much
Has long ago been the subject
Of such lively dispute, where the inhabitants
Are the same people at heart,
As they always were, but who
Equally believe they are not;
Into a land between two worlds,
Our road hugs ripening fields,
Of calculated barley,
Past neat farms cherished
In all their corners;
Undisturbed by the wind
Of our passage, those we glimpse,
The farmer on his tractor,

The boy walking a dog
Beside a meandering burn
Seem indifferent, and understandably so,
To our noisy concern
To be somewhere else.

Any journey, if reflected upon,
Might make us think
About whether we really need
To do what we do, to move about
With such grim determination
Not to linger in one place
Any longer than we need to be.
Not long ago—a lifetime or two—
People went nowhere, staying
In their village, in their place,
From childhood to old age;
Six miles was a long way away
In those days; one hundred miles
An awfully long journey,
Undertaken heart in mouth
Over all the unknowns it involved.

I knew a man who spoke of another
Who never went anywhere:
He lived on a Scottish island,
And the sea lay between
Him and Scotland itself;
If the sea was there, he said,
It was there for a reason.

Was he photographed?
Did he ever look into the lens
Of an enthusiast with a camera?
Probably; and if he did, did he look happy,
Did he look as if he wanted
To be somewhere else?
Probably not, unlike ourselves,
To whom islands have long since
Ceased to be a problem,
And to whom whole seas are nothing at all.

Four brief hours of railway now stand
Between sedate Edinburgh and sprawling London;
We fly to New York before lunch,
Even Australia, these days, can be reached
Without the need to pack pyjamas.
Rapidly our world contracts,
Vainly we try to slow the pace,
To sit in our chairs, quite still,
Watching the sky, counting the clouds;
Though cherished things, old things
Wrought in a slower time,
With all the love that personal making
Can give to that which is made—
Those things remind us, describe
The nature of journeys made
But no longer made, the world
As it still might be, had we the time.

Here are two poems about journeys on trains. The first describes arrival in London. People flock into the city, each with his or her purpose: a day at work, a visit, an assignation—there are many reasons why people converge on a city. For some, the moment of arrival is significant and exciting; for the city, it is nothing much, a daily event, repeated and repeated.

THE TRAIN ARRIVING AT PLATFORM TWO

We are now approaching King's Cross Station,
And bluebells climb a bank; ground elder too,
Beneath sycamores unplanned, seedlings
That had arrived from somewhere woodier;
Under a bridge, defaced by painted scrawls,
To the platform itself, where a man, alone,
Clad in dowdy clothing looks uncertain
As to which train to board;
                    up above
A London sky, pale blue, unclouded,
Poked into by arrogant buildings,
Products of an architectural ego
Craving attention like a teenager;
A clutter of roofs and solar panels
Begging the sun to visit; distant chimneys;
A city that has seen it all,
                    and more,
The hum of outrageous empire;
The smell of trade, moments of decision;

This city says: come join my multitudes,
There is not water nor air enough
For all of you, but come to this spectacle
And marvel, spend your money,
And return to a place where others
Know your name, your looks,
And all the failings you'd prefer
Not to tell us about;
                    not that we mind:
We hear and see too much to care,
For each day, unfailing, it begins again,
Equal in sunshine as in rain,
Others come, and do the things they must,
The sad, the crooked, and the just,
The weather comes and goes, all right,
The crowds, the traffic, and the night.

And here is a play on Edward Thomas's haunting poem, "Adelstrop," so utterly memorable for its pastoral invocation and the name of the railway siding. This poem deals with the kind of persistent announcements in railway stations that would have been so unnecessary in Thomas's day: "If you see anything that does not look right, report it." We know what they mean, but do they really mean *this*? The poem begins on a note of sympathy for those modern Dantean wraiths, commuters.

ADELSTROP REVISITED

Familiar enough to each other,
After years of silent journeys
Unaware, though, of who exactly
Is who, or what brings each
To this daily shared procession,
They hear but do not hear
The official voice announces:
Should you see anything
That does not look right,
Report it. No one does,
And yet everything, to my eye,
Looks wrong, and therefore is not right;
It is not right that people
Should be indifferent
To one another; should not know
Who the other is, nor care, it seems;
It is not right that so many lives
Should pass in this way, bound

To a Sisyphean schedule
Of never-ending travel;
It is not right, it seems,
That there should not be time
To look at the sky, to stop
And walk slowly and breathe
The morning air before
Staleness sets in. None of that
Looks right; I report it,
And wait for a response,
And wait, and all the birds
Of Oxfordshire return and briefly sing.

Air travel has none of the romance of rail. In the past that might not have been so: Antoine de Saint Exupéry wrote *Night Flight* and Cecil Day-Lewis penned a long poem about two early aviators who flew all the way to Australia. Now, however, the antiseptic and cumbersome jets that heave themselves into the air have very little romance about them and are generally to be endured rather than celebrated. Part of the problem, of course, is the soullessness that hangs about air transport. There are so many dimensions to that, but one is language. If you listen to the way pilots and cabin crew address their passengers, you will quickly see how dry and without salience is the language they use. What if a pilot were to be a poet, and spoke poetically to the passengers?

THE LANGUAGE OF PILOTS

They speak with high authority,
Ailerons and wings responsive
To their touch: their words
Are functional too, but
Why, I wonder, should a pilot
Not be a poet too, and say:

"We now descend at last
Through banks of cloud,
White fields as wide
As any ocean, at least when viewed
From where we are,
At least when viewed
From this suspended point,

For it is Bernoulli's principle
That lifts and keeps us here,
Between the patient earth below
And this empty, soaring sky.

Ladies and gentlemen, rain
Falls in distant veils;
Look from your windows
To the starboard side
Of this metal tube
We call an aircraft;
Look out there, and see
The rain, the grey-white
Shafts of rain; do you know
That those wisps of cloud
You see up above
Are crystals of ice, falling
Like gossamer? Did you
Know that? Now please
About your waists
Affix the belts; you must,
As slowly towards the earth we drop,
To land's embrace,
(Your belts adjust);
We are a little late, but what
Are a few minutes, nothing more,
Here and there? Not much, I think.
Goodbye, and take with you
The things you brought,
Your few possessions. Goodbye

Until we meet again,
And once more we carry you,
On wings of steel, on wings of steel,
To places you would wish to go;
Goodbye, dear friends, it matters not
Whether you're a member of
The loyalty scheme we've got;
We love you all, as parents
Love their children equally,
Remember that, and please come back.
Goodbye again, and cabin crew
Unbar the doors, let light be seen,
Secure what needs securing and
Cross check, whatever that might mean.
Goodbye: for soon these great engines
On landing will be silenced, as will I."

Travelling by air, you see very little; there are clouds, of course, but their attraction wanes after a while. Down below, the earth is too distant to reveal much, although the Himalayas or the Rockies may engage our attention. A journey by road, however, is a different matter, and even in a uniform landscape there are always signs to be noticed. While travelling between Los Angeles and Santa Barbara some years ago, I saw a road sign that immediately sent me to my notebook and to the writing of this poem in the car. (I was not driving).

COLLEGE OF HYPNOTHERAPY,
NEXT RIGHT
(a sign on the highway, in Los Angeles, near Hollywood)

This winter sunshine
Attenuated but still warm
Is the democratic air through
Which the gliding limos
And the working trucks
Move equally; bare hills
Describe the outer limits
To this Los Angeles landscape,
Indicate the boundaries
Of the possible in a place
Where anything can be done;
For this is where illusion
Has its kingdom; where things
Can mean what you
Want them to mean, and more;

Where the paying customer
Is only too ready and willing
To think that being fooled
Is satisfactory entertainment.

The autumnal fall of leaves
Is not an issue here;
Along the banks of this
Interminable highway
Are eucalypts, Tipu trees,
Riots of bougainvillea,
All asserting that perpetual
Summer pertains in this south;
Even, one suspects, the lotus itself
Blooms here, tended
For personal use, of course.

Somewhere, under the glitter
Of distant gleaming towers,
Somewhere under the acres
Of quite undifferentiated roofs,
There is an old history here,
Of conquest, dispossession,
Of forgotten missions,
Of old and modern empires
Locked in a tawdry struggle
For the right to name;
And now Mexico seems
Ever closer than it was,
Spanish seeps into the interstices

Of a protestant life
That's never been all that happy
In the sun; kisses and softens
Anglo-Saxon place names
That need only a vowel
To make the transition
To sympathy and the guitar.

The signs flash past:
City of a Thousand Oaks:
First exit ahead;
I count only six, planted
Along an unexceptional
Concrete mall; nine hundred
And more must be elsewhere,
As many promises are
In a place that assures you
Your future is attainable.

And then a sign that warns
College of Hypnotherapy,
Next Right. This says so much:
You will leave the road,
Close your eyes and let
Your mind drift as it will;
Replace thought with no thought,
Listen to my voice, this
Is the College of Hypnotherapy
Speaking to you; next right;
Now, don't put change off;

Keep driving, do not flinch,
You can be better, you can stop
The things you want to stop;
Believe in me, and in this sign:
College of Hypnotherapy, Next Right.

In India, keep a sharp eye out for signs, which may say so much. "Quality provisions for ever" was the message of a sign I spotted in Kerala.

QUALITY PROVISIONS FOR EVER

Here on the road between this place and the next,
With South India to the north, and to the south
A sea of fishing boats and hazy distances,
Shops and houses create a wavering line
Of unharmonious architecture,
Buildings that bear no relation
The one to the other, save for optimism:
A two-storey construction
Proclaims itself a tower;
A concrete box, its windows shuttered,
Is none other than The Excellence Hotel;
An eye surgeon lists his qualifications
In large and easily readable type—
A foretaste, perhaps, of what surgery
Might achieve; from time to time
A temple promotes its special god,
Or a Latin church its saint—
Religion is tolerant
In these latitudes, welcomes
Each new vision of how
We came to be where we are;
An astrologer offers detailed charts
Of a future that we universally

Hope will be better than today,
With its landscape of disappointments;
That sense of betterment
Is what enables people here
To tolerate, to believe
It's worth continuing; worth bearing too
An unremitting and unforgiving sun;
Traffic, the demands of extended family,
Dishonest bureaucrats, the unattainable
Life portrayed in films and in their posters,
Where the hero is so much better looking
Than anyone one knows, and dancing
Is resolution and solution, all in one.

And then a sign that says:
Quality provisions for ever;
And that is what I wish my friends,
For whom I could wish, I suppose,
Reciprocated love, unconditional fame,
A place in the history books,
A job for life, with pension,
A lottery win or an unexpected award;
But, knowing these unlikely,
I wish instead something
That we all can understand
And is not wildly improbable:
Quality provisions for ever,
The simplest sign, as is often the case,
Goes to the heart of what we know
We all would have:

Quality provisions for ever.
Enough said; signs may fall silent now,
None will match its understanding
Of human needs and hopes;
None will deride it, none would
Say I wish for something else.

While travelling in high country in Victoria, I passed a sign saying "Grumpy and Ange." The owners of the plot had their names on the gate—a common thing in rural Australia. I imagined the lives of these two—another Grumpy and Ange—not the real ones, but who they might be.

NOT RUS IN URBE BUT SUBURBIA IN RURE

A mountainside of eucalypts,
Survivors, successors, of fires,
Clinging impossibly sometimes
To the thin soil of rocky places,
Roots in the interstices of rocks,
Reaching, probing, into a sky
That is high and dizzy;
And all about there is a dryness
Redolent of parsimonious rain,
Of storms that blow and threaten
But come to nothing much,
And yet, in this dry landscape
There is a majesty, an iron-bound
Dignity, an emptiness,
A chorus of echoes, the lonely score
Of a wide continent, its past
Destroyed by implacable nature
As often as it recreates itself;
But then, suddenly, prosaic human settlement
Intrudes on this sparse purity,

As here, unexpectedly, a sign
Announces the home of Grumpy and Ange:
Grumpy, he who ran a hardware store,
For years uncounted, who complained
About his customers and found fault
With politicians, priests, and policemen,
Wrote letters to the press
About this and that, was never satisfied
With the response, was grumpy;
But Ange—oh, Ange, now there's one
Who never found fault, helped others,
Sympathised, baked lamington cakes
For good causes, helped grounded birds
Recover flight, made others better;
A true angel, Ange, and were real angels
To pause in flight across these skies,
Were to look down and notice Ange,
Would see her as one of their own, elect;
Would not see him, with his gaze
On the things that are unsatisfactory;
These heavenly beings would wave to Ange
And then pass on, into the clouds,
Into the white unlimited sky
And the silences that infuse the sky.

Which leads naturally to more about angels—beings in which I do not believe, but that are believed in by many—possibly the majority of people.

A TYPOLOGY OF ANGELS

Of all pursuits of the human mind
Few will be stranger than angelology,
The study of angels by those enthusiasts
Who have never found the thing they seek
But who, in most cases, one imagines,
So want the elusive quarry to exist;
Never having seen angels in person
Is a condition in which most of us,
The uncommitted ones, would imagine
Ourselves to be; this does not preclude
Detailed knowledge of how angels
Appear, and what, if only allowed to exist,
They might wish to achieve;
Angels see themselves, we're told,
As messengers—or that, at least,
Is how they were first employed,
A subsidiary role, then, carrying
The words of others, dispensing
An announcement here, a warning there,
Vouchsafers of the occasional vision;
Bearers, not composers, of words
That we'd do well not to ignore.
Choosing an angel to make your announcement

Inevitably guarantees an audience,
And painters of angels, iconographers,
Always include a company of listeners.

So it is that when an angel appears,
Those who witness his arrival
Are ready to listen—and wouldn't you
Be rapt were a winged delivery man
To set foot on your doorstep
With an air of having something to say?

In time, their province expanded:
From messenger to guardian
Was but a small step;
Now they stood behind
The one to whom they were allocated
And deflected the things
That would harm their charge;
An arrow, a sword,
Simple misfortune could all
Be turned aside, avoided,
By a skilful angelic parry
Or a protective, though unseen, hand.

In the iconography of angels
Guardian angels are portrayed
With their hands on the shoulders
Of those whom they protect;
I like a hand on my shoulder,
Feel comforted by the humanity of it;

How reassuring it must be
To close your eyes in sleep
In the knowledge that one
So attired and winged, some acolyte of Gabriel
Or Michael, perhaps, stands at your head
And at your feet. To be not alone
Is an ambition of us all;
To have powerful friends
Even more so; if it allows us
To believe in at least something
Unlikely, then surely
We might permit ourselves this,
An innocent belief that harms nobody,
Has no carbon footprint
And, most importantly, makes nobody cry.
A belief in angels speaks to our desire
For the world to be less arbitrary,
And subject to a certain sort of justice;
That the defeated should be exalted,
That the lonely should be granted a friend,
That the heart-injured should be healed—
And feel a little better now.
That angels should be on our side;
Are these such impossible wishes?
Are these such illusory desires?

Household gods are another manifestation of the human desire for the sacred. The Romans were enthusiastic hosts to household gods, which also appear in other spiritual traditions. The real deities behind the idols may be imaginary—or wishful thinking— but that does not stop people from having shrines to their household gods—shrines in which the offerings will be kept fresh, sanctifying that space most would wish to sanctify: the home. Of course the requests made of household gods may be presumptuous and too much for any minor deity to accomplish—but people are optimists, and will still try.

HOUSEHOLD GODS

Household gods, though you are asked
Too frequently to perform the task
Of blessing, I still would plead
In charity you'll intercede
On our behalf, grant private wishes
Optimistic and auspicious:
Bless eggs, omelettes, and potatoes,
The gatherers of herbs and cultivators,
Bless morning brightness and the night,
The darkness and the warming light,
The gentle winds, the patient land,
The mountains and the desert sand;
Bless those I love and those who may
Listen to what I have to say.
Bless those who in each other's arms
Find haven from all ill and harm.

Dear household gods, I've not got through
The list of things that you should do;
But remember me, if you can
And explain the ways of gods to man;
I, at least, will then believe
How it is you can relieve
The pain we feel, in our being
Our simple selves; while you, all knowing,
Will help us in our daily growing.
We turn to you, as to a friend,
And light a candle to that end.

Nowhere, of course, has more gods than India, where the deities of Hinduism are believed to be uncountable. Household gods are common there still, and every hamlet will have a shrine of some sort, however humble. One of the most striking sights of the southern state of Kerala, where Marxism and Christianity have both been influential, is, beside the roadside, a bust of Karl Marx on one corner, on the next a Christian image placed there for travellers, and not far away a small Ganesh garlanded with fresh flowers. There are many places in India that are holy to at least some local adherents of a faith, and this is especially true of rivers, which may be holy to millions. The Narmada River is one such holy river, less well known to foreigners than the Ganges, but very important in Hinduism. I noticed on its banks a line of small statues of holy cows, and then some real, nonchalant goats.

HOLY RIVER

When gods decide to inhabit a river
So priests and builders of temples
May call it holy, they hardly care
Whether it flows from east to west,
Whether it drains into this or that
Ocean, nor whether waterfalls and rocks
Interrupt it here and there;
These things interest geographers
And merchants, but fail to affect
The evident suitability of a river
To wash away sins, to make the lame
Sounder of limb, the unhappy
Less soul-injured in their loneliness.

What matters is the presence of banks
And paths that lead to them,
And landings, perhaps, where boats
May disembark the chattering pilgrims;
What matters are shady canopies
Under which those who assemble
May talk of the miracles they
Have only just failed to witness:
It is true, I think, that the miraculous
Usually happens to somebody else,
Somebody we almost met,
But missed by minutes, whose deliverance
Was witnessed by others, credible
Each, with no reason to exaggerate
Or plainly invent. A holy river
Needs a stage on which to assert
Its holiness, needs an audience
Of those who are anxious enough to believe,
Needs the vocal endorsement
Of gods and those who put their trust in gods.

Here, at Maheshwar, on the Narmada,
A river where Ganga herself, splendid
Patroness of a more famous river
Will come to bathe, a band of pilgrims,
One of many, enters the water
Watched by others; the sun above
Is merciless at noon, reflected heat
From sculpted stone makes goats languid;
At night the candles, each in a tiny boat

Of waxed and circular cardboard,
Are lit and launched; *send me a husband,*
Grant me a wife, relieve my pain,
Bring me wealth and all the things
That wealth can bring; forget
The pleas of others and attend to mine;
Tolerant, the water continues on its way,
Bearer, on its surface, of these human wishes,
Happy enough to dispense to each
A sense of belonging, a moment of hope.

In Rajasthan, I travelled on a rough track through mustard fields. In the field before me was a small temple, as if dropped down, in the middle of nowhere—or planted perhaps?

MUSTARD FIELD, RAJASTHAN

Sometimes, when you plant a field of mustard
In Rajasthan, under the gaze of a mountain,
Something unexpected may grow—
Seeds, even from a reliable source,
Looking much the same, as seeds do,
May grow an unusual crop:
A temple, perhaps, or, as here,
A small temple with a slightly larger one
A short distance away, the length
Of two priests, laid head to toe,
A home for comfortable gods,
Those familiars of hearth and home,
Who may wait a long time for an offering,
And never complain that it's too small.
You may not expect a temple to emerge,
Believing such things are made
By builders, masons, architects;
Seeing it here, then, may reveal
Your lack of faith in the occurrence
Of unusual and beautiful miracles,
May persuade you of their possibility,
That's all; that's all I'm saying.

So it is in life, a surprise
May follow upon what you do;
A kiss planted on a cheek
May grow into a love affair;
A kind word, not meaning much at all,
May become a jewelled encomium;
A tiny gesture of understanding
May end a feud, may change a life,
May be a healing balm;
A sprig of simile, uttered unknowing,
May make us cry buckets, as we all have done,
For what we have lost, for yesterday,
For what we never knew we had.

Do not be surprised, then,
If in your mustard field
An unplanned temple grows.

Elsewhere in Rajasthan, while visiting a site of an ancient settlement now in the care of the archaeological authorities, I encountered a metal sign, set on a plinth of stone, with a conservation message for the visitor. This sign said, simply: "Protect your heritage and feel glorious."

The site was overrun with monkeys, aggressive defenders of their space. One temple here concealed another.

FEEL GLORIOUS

Beyond one temple, past carved pillars,
Another temple, in the middle distance,
Of sandstone, sits just beneath the hill
That rises rock-strewn, sheer
Above the ruins of this ancient town;
Round the corner, concealed,
Older than both these temples
A third temple may be hidden,
A temple to which no path
Currently leads, forgotten
By priests, by guides, by lovers
Who come for privacy;
A temple may be in the care
Of mute stone statues,
Or of ill-tempered priests,
May be colonised by chattering monkeys
Or birds resting in its eaves;
A gift to the priest may bring
A lifting of priestly mood;

A cautious prediction
Of good fortune, of love, of all
Those human things we long to find,
We yearn to have; the larger the gift
The greater the measure
Of good fortune predicted.
Bells will chime, emaciated goats will
Move across exhausted fields;
A government sign proclaims:
Protect your heritage
And feel glorious.

Public signs tell us so much—often about things on which the original sign-maker did not intend to make any comment. On the island of Martinique, I visited the public gardens where the mistranslation of a sign accidentally gave us advice on the conduct of our lives.

DO NOT LEAN AGAIN
(a sign in the botanical gardens in Martinique)

We know what it means,
But what it says is:
Do not lean again.
That is all:
Do not lean again.

Not all of us are confident
Of the vertical, the unsupported state;
At times we need to lean
And will be forgiven the weakness
That makes necessary the leaning;
At times we are allowed
To look for support
From those about us, the stronger,
The haler and heartier,
The more leaned-against than leaning,
Who are more securely founded,
Have roots, a sense of who they are,
And will invariably remain erect;
A balanced world allows such symbiosis,

Pardons instability, allows the weak
To look for a broader shoulder,
A steadying hand, a sympathetic haven.
But there are limits; *do not lean again:*
When you have just finished
Leaning on one, do not transfer
Too quickly to another; stand up straight
And face the world yourself
Before you try to lean again.
Do not expect there always to be
Somebody else on whom to lean,
Do not lean again lest you discover
The person on whom you lean
Is no longer there, or has found
That he, too, has a need to lean.
Do not lean again, do not expect
The same thing to work twice;
Do not lean again lest you find
That support against which you lean
Gives way; a fence may conceal
An abyss waiting to devour
Those who lean again; a vertical drop,
A nothingness, some worse place
Than that in which you find yourself;
Do not lean again; no, *do not lean again.*

And on the same island, in the capital, I came across this sign—
the first time I have seen such a message. It was both stern and
unambiguous: *Ne pas uriner ici!*

NE PAS
(a sign on a wall in Fort-de-France, Martinique)

It is a pity that civic authorities
Should feel compelled to be so specific;
One might imagine that the bourgeoisie
Would hardly need to be so instructed.
Yet this sign is explicitly not for them:
This is for the seditious, the disrespectful,
The sort of people who deface library books,
Fail to stand for the National Anthem
(Or dance to it, just to show),
Who avoid the agents of the treasury—and the police;
Such people are always with us,
Lower the civic tone, make it necessary
To have signs such as this.
Will they obey it? I'll bet they don't:
Such types ignore notices,
Lead their lives just as they wish to lead them,
Pay scant attention, are happy, defy
The sound advice of their betters
And die unrepentant, full of years, relieved.

A Scottish Four Seasons

SPRING

For spring is neither one thing
Nor the other; spring may make
A convincing statement,
A claim of growth and emergence,
But may change its mind
And revert—like some timid creature
Creeping out from its burrow
To find the world still frozen
And then retreating for a few last
Days of hibernation.

In the north of Scotland,
Sometimes in June
They'll still be waiting for spring,
Not that they complain:
Spring will come, they say,
Even if only after summer has begun.

Spring inspires new starts;
The sweeping away of things
That have cluttered the house too long;
The polishing of floors and banisters,
The abandonment of sluggish ideas
And notions that the light of day
Makes look so unattractive, so last-year.
And prompts some searching questions:
Should I wear a different tie?
Should I abandon workday shoes

For something racier?
Should I find new friends
And think new thoughts?
These the questions
Raised by spring, but rarely answered.

SUMMER

Rewarded now with summer calm,
Two lovers lie upon a Scottish hill
Beneath a sky that deepest blue
Bereft of limit to its end;
Oh, listen now, my dearest one
To all the things I'd wish for you:
A hundred lovely days like this,
A sun that lingers, hardly sets
And evenings that are barely dark,
The briefest pause before the dawn.

Behind them as he speaks these words,
The slow currents of the Sound of Mull
Move past the island's shores;
There is so much to love in this country,
When it is like this, and is at peace,
When its crouching hills
Are the guardians of these hidden glens
Where heather and Scots pines
Remind us of evenings past
When the world was less a place of wrong,
When love, not distrust, was the key
In which the nations sang their song.

May soft winds blow about your head,
May sun caress your tender cheeks,
May tears of gentle rain then wash
The marks of fretful care away;
May you remember from this day
Good resolutions and great plans,
Our promises once made believed,
The sharing of our private hopes,
In letters that are signed with love,
With secret names, with pencilled signs.

AUTUMN

Look, the migrating birds
Are leaving us, small souls
That brave three thousand miles
To Africa, to warmth;
They populate the sky,
They take the last
Attributes of summer;
They are gone, and now
The winds will have them,
Their journey starts
In the knowledge that this,
Like the seasons, has to be.

Autumn is a time of reflection;
Of the making of lists,
Of books to be read now
That the nights are drawing in;
Of letters to be written,
Friends to be remembered,
The things they said
To be thought about further.
Perhaps, in short, to think
About what it is that makes
This life so precious
Of what it is that breaks the heart.

WINTER

That there should be winter, that this hard light
Should fall over a December Scotland,
Should make the sea grey, like steel, and the land itself
A rock rising from metalled water;
That there should be empty skies,
Free of protecting cloud, too cold
Even for that; that there should be
A vapour trail of some great jet heading west
To the colder shores of Greenland, Labrador,
Northern neighbours to us, distant cousins
In our marginality and our pursuit of fish;
That all this should be in a land that in summer
Is so soft and wet with drifting veils of rain
And filled with deer and clouds of midges
And the rich fecundity of ploughed fields
That will yield gold barley and whisky
Beyond the barley—

Scotland is a country of attenuated light,
And temperate-to-inhospitable seasons;
Freshness and cold skies lie behind
All our signs, our ways of being;
I sometimes wish, I confess, for a life spent
In the scent of wild thyme and olive trees,
For evenings when one might stroll
Slowly about a square and watch pigeons
Launch themselves into Italian air
From some tower dreamed up

By some High Renaissance imagination;
That, though, is not where we are from
Or where we are destined to be;
Our place is north, our natural gravity
That of a land that is an afterthought
To Europe, a land that comes late
To so many of the parties it's been invited to,
But which we love with all our heart,
With all our heart.

Winter doesn't make us better, then, or worse,
But enables us to find ourselves again,
Because it forces us to be quiet, obliges us
To listen to the coursing of our own blood;
Winter reminds us that warmth
Is not something we find naturally,
Some gift of munificent nature, but must be made;
That we should make in Scotland
A small place of warmth, a small country
Of kindness to others, of brotherhood,
Is what our poets have been striving to say
Since they first gave voice to song.
That we might find this, in winter,
In a troubled world, is a local miracle,
To warm the heart, to warm the heart.

Interlude:

Seven Sonnets

The sonnet, a formal verse form, is still capable of commenting on contemporary life.

Its favoured subjects, of course, don't change: life, love, introspection, constancy and inconstancy, and age . . .

I. SIXTY TALKS TO EIGHTEEN

Unfearless, at eighteen, of gravity and time,
Of mirrors, of insurance, and the cold
Facts of economics, they show that old
Indifference of the young to the actuarial
Warnings of the strong chance that passion
In its firm and quite inevitable fashion
Will falter and will fade, as arterial
Silting slows the blood, and the human colt
Becomes the drayhorse; why should they
Pause to think of what others say
They should do? It's not their fault
The world is as it is, our self-created mess.

We've one thing, though, that they've not got:
We can with ease reflect on what is not.

11. EIGHTEEN REPLIES TO SIXTY

Please forgive me if I did not see
You standing there, there comes a stage
When visibility is quite lost by age;
Noticed by others, although not by me,
You fade into a background
Of things that while they may be there
Are not in any true sense in the here
And now; I wonder, have you found
Your invisibility a blessing in truth,
As freed from the onerous need to bother
What you look like, you think of other
Ways of recapturing lost youth?

I understand that you should feel bereft
Now there is so little time that's left.

III. FORTY INTERVENES,
REMEMBERS HORACE

Not half bad, friends, is this sensation
Of having got this far along
Without getting it too badly wrong,
And finding now that one's situation
Is reasonably comfortable, not bad,
Married to one who'll plainly do,
Looked after, smiled at, there are few
Who'll not proclaim that husband, dad,
Are roles that bring a certain joy
At this particular stage of life,
No stomach is needed for the strife
You haven't experienced since a boy.

Remember, then, the poet Horace,
Whose simple life, with wine, brought solace.

Horace, of course, would be an advocate of staying put. If he were
to contemplate our modern life he might say: why are you so keen
to travel?

IV. ADVENTURE AND UNCERTAINTY

Embarking on a journey without maps
Against the currents or on a troubled sea
Reminds us, if we need it, to be free
Involves that tricky word that is *perhaps*;
Perhaps it's better to remain just where
You started from, yes, an undistinguished place,
But going nowhere, after all, is no disgrace;
You know, at least, just who and what is there.
Few people like the view that they're too small
To lead the hero's life: that lengthy trail
Odysseus bravely followed cannot fail
To inspire those who've never lived at all.

But courting danger, we might all agree,
Is not the only way of being free.

The Horatian philosophy might also stress humility—a virtue that seems to be becoming rare in our age of self-aggrandisement and self-celebration. Look at your achievements—remember, they are not just yours. We achieve what we achieve on the shoulders of others.

V. IT TAKES A VILLAGE TO
RAISE A CHILD

Mozart thought—or should have—if he did not,
The music was always there, all he had to do
Was write it down; I imagine few
Of those who think great thoughts, a lot
Of us, after all, no false modesty,
Should tell us not to claim the praise
For what we do; there are many ways
Of diffidence, yet it seems to me
The words "I've done this all" are rarely true
The things that we achieve, or most
Of them are that, and no more than a boast
Of what we once believed that we could do.

Remember, then, that without others' aid
No art, nor any *urbs* was ever made.

And finally, love—the subject that sustained one of the greatest collections of verse of any age—Shakespeare's sonnets. King James VI of Scotland (King James I of England) suffered in his early life under a stern tutor, George Buchanan. Then suddenly light and colour came into his life, and the boy king fell in love with his male cousin, Esmé Stuart, who came to Scotland from France. When Esmé was sent back to France, James was bereft.

VI. KING JAMES VI OF SCOTLAND REFLECTS ON THE LOSS OF HIS ONLY FRIEND WHEN YOUNG

Cousin, you came into my life too late
To be the one to teach me how to see
How strange it is to be a slave of Fate,
Even though men should subjects be to me.
But what you taught me—that I'll always hold
More precious than the gifts of high estate,
Those are base metal, while your words are gold
Displayed in letters large at Heaven's gate;
A gentle look, a secret touch, a smile,
Given free and by outsider's hand unbidden,
Will count for more than any trick or wile
Or words in which a heart of ice is hidden.

Now you are gone, you have put out the light
That bathed my days in sun, that banished night.

But at least he had experienced love. And that is a consolation in circumstances where love is locked out, or lost, or unreciprocated. The conclusion in the final two lines of the following poem is that we will never get another to love us by revealing to the one we love that we are miserable without him or her. That never works. Even trees prefer to have two doves than one.

VII. LOVE UNFORGOTTEN

When I felt lonely I would go around
Lost in a crowd of those I did not know,
Hoping to hear the once familiar sound,
The voice of one who claimed to love me so;
But listened in vain just as I listen still,
For you to utter, to evoke my name,
Knowing the ear's a trickster and often will
Contrive to make other people sound the same;
You needed do no more than write to me,
You needed do no more than make a call;
Writing costs nothing, email's almost free,
My sorrow, though, I think counts not at all.

An injured heart does not engender love,
No sheltering tree will want a single dove.

Of the Animals

PRIMATE COUSINS

Like us, they walk upon two legs,
And use their hands for tasks
That we perform, too,
In ways that are not different;

Like us, they favour fruit as well
And peel it in those ways
We use to separate
Inner food from outer cover;

Like us, they are sensitive to gesture,
And live in company,
Governed by their customs,
Have their leaders and arguments;

Like us, they need food and shelter,
Are vulnerable in sleep,
Play games with their offspring,
And hope for better times ahead;

Like us, they have their memories,
And a sense of a past,
May gently groom and preen,
In friendships that will last a primate life.

THE GENTLENESS OF WHALES

For the whales move slowly,
Larger than any other life,
Announced in the waters
With their plumes of spray,
Exhalations from lungs
Large beyond imagination;
As gentle as the touch
Of early morning sun;
For there are none like them,
None who have their dignity.

Above them green waters
Enfold and embrace
These creatures of another time;
When the space of the world
Was sufficient for Behemoth;
For there are none like them,
None who are as gentle.

Listen to their calls, songs
Of one to another, of things
That of each the other
Would wish to know;
Of the green depths and the waters
Where kin meets kin
Across the empty miles;
They flourish above wide forests
Of waving kelp, in caverns

Of liquid blue beyond
Our human envisioning;
For there are none like them
In the waters of this earth;
None who can replace them.

ELEPHANTS

They are grey shapes in the trees,
They are like moving rocks,
They are the wide-legged ones,
The bearers of ivory, the small-eyed,
The trumpeters, with ears like sails,
The heavy-footed.
    They are the ones who reproach us
For what we have done, for taking
Their world away from them;
They are the ones in whom the dignity of great forms
Is most resolutely and finally expressed.

You cannot understand our words,
Although your brains have memories, like ours,
And you mourn your dead, as we do;
So when we ask of you your forgiveness
For our history of wanton slaughter
Of elephant kind, our words are lost,
Indecipherable, lost to your loyal heart,
Lost in the silence of your shrinking forests,
Your dwindling home.

KANGAROOS

You occupy a land of reds and browns,
Of flame and water, and hard rock;
You move through eucalyptus scrub
And tinder grass, across a land so thirsty
That it aches; and yet you yourself are grey
And red and soft, and take your tiny young
Into the warm comfort of a maternal pouch,
Bound and leap across a landscape
Bathed in birdsong; the kookaburra,
The pink galah your minstrels;
Under these stars, dipping and wheeling
Through their southern night, you sleep on dust,
Part of our dreams, part of our symbolism
You cross small segments of the sky.

THE DUNG BEETLE

Onerous your task,
You tiny Sisyphus,
Condemned, like him,
To move your boulder
Without cease;
Unaware of any
Easier life—it is not right
That the labours of one
Should be amusement
For others; I'm sorry,
I do not mean to laugh
At the heroic, the purposeful.
May you get to your destination
Just as we wish to get to ours.

TORTOISE

Heavy with years, laden with caution
And carapace, the tortoise moves across the land
Weighed with all the statistics of how long
It would take such a creature to walk
The average island from end to end—
Several years, no doubt.
Scientists measure the dauntingly long
In the years a beam of light
Would take to travel such a route;
Tortoise years would make those distances
Seem even greater, even less imaginable,
More like the reality of infinite time.

CHEETAH

Fast as untethered wind, whipping
The branches of trees and grass
Flat against their natural posture,
Fast as high cirrus racing
Through echoing limitless sky,
Fast as a dancing shadow
In its moment of passing,
This mottled creature
Is perfect in all its aerodynamics,
Fleeter of foot than any athlete,
Overtaker of every creature
That ever fancied itself a runner;
Who is for some no more
Than a yellow streak, a temporary
Blur of colour, easily missed,
For its prey, their last mistake,
The last consequence of slowness.

POLAR BEAR

Anxious, lest ice floes move
To carry him from the familiar,
Aware, somehow, and yet
Not understanding why the world
Is becoming smaller;
Hungry for food that once
Was plentiful and now
Eludes him—a bear, white as ice,
And now as susceptible,
Lives shortening days
In spite of light.

CROCODILE

Not expecting to be loved
But marvellous nonetheless,
A survivor of an ancient line,
And proud of it, uncaring,
Of what those who do not bask
On sand banks should think
Of those who do.

Crocodylus niloticus! Crocodylus niloticus!
Crocodylus niloticus et horrificus!

See the teeth, and eyes
Not intended to convey emotion
As other eyes might do,
But appraising you as breakfast;
Yet we admire you, crocodile,
From that vantage point
That is often best of all:
A safe distance; a safe distance.

Crocodylus niloticus! Crocodylus niloticus!
Crocodylus niloticus et horrificus!

LION

I had a dream about a lion,
A lion that walked in morning light,
That felt the wind upon its mane,
That stirred in shadows of the night.

I had a dream about a lion,
That came so softly to my side,
And coughed as lions are apt to do,
And rubbed against me its soft hide

That smelled of lion and air and death;
And the great sky was white and empty.
We would embrace this tawny sinew;
Would stroll with him in companionship;
But no, he is imperial, and walks in majesty;
Remember he is *not* a constitutional monarch.

SMALL, INSIGNIFICANT ANTELOPE

They run here and there, with no purpose
That we, at least, can ascertain,
Moved by pure panic; perhaps these small antelope
Would see themselves
As stately herds of zebras, no less,
Moving liquid stripes across savannah.
Or wildebeest, or anything more impressive
Than themselves, than minor antelope;
But how clever of you—to panic at the world.

GIRAFFE, ZEBRA

Those who know their way
About the species will never
Mistake one zebra for another,
A Masai giraffe
For a reticulated giraffe,
A common plains zebra
For Grévy's Zebra,
Even if zebras themselves
May sometimes get that wrong
And interbreed, mixing up the stripes
In moments of passion;
We may all make that mistake—
Those of us who are not zebras
As much as those who are;
Love and anger are equally
Capable of misting our vision;
A cool head enables us
To work out what is what,
To realise that things are not always
What they claim, sometimes quite loudly,
Not to be.

OUR WORLD, THEIR WORLD

They are our companions, the animals,
The ones with whom we share this space,
This spinning treasury of air and water,
We used to think our kingdoms were quite separate,
Split by language and the reasoning mind;
No more; they have their reason, the animals,
They have their language—the call of whales
Across a thousand miles of water,
The territorial challenges of birds,
The bellow of pain, of loss—a language
We have never really listened to,
But which we hear today; listen: the language
Of our brothers and our sisters.
We have only one home,
And that is a common one;
We have only one life,
And that is a precious one;
There is only one way,
And that is the healing one.

Of Love & Longing

The weather that comes in from the Atlantic touches Scotland first on its islands. This is Scotland's first defence, as the mountains meet the clouds. Rain falls in veils—tears that remind us of the tears we shed for the beauty of this country and for the feelings of loss and regret that we all experience at some point in our lives.

LOVE OVER SCOTLAND

But what do I wish for you?
Wish for love over Scotland,
Like tears of rain;
That is enough.

ON CLOUDS OVER MULL: A LOVE SONG

White the shifting veils of rain
That fall like tears, like tears, so white,
And soft upon your cheek, my dear,
So soft and wet upon your cheek;
And Mull stands guard against
The green sea, stands guard
Against the green sea.

And if our hearts will have to weep,
As all hearts will, and ours must do,
Then we shall shed on this soft isle
These human tears, like tears of rain
That fall so soft upon the land
So gentle in their quiet regret
For what is not, and cannot be,
For what is not, and cannot be.

NOCTURNAL BLESSING

Full and forgiving, the tolerant moon now hangs
Above the world of each, its gentle light
Is that by which absurd nocturnal roles
Are spun and acted out in private dreams;
Visions and hope come easily to sleepers,
Consign the laws of physics, for some hours at least,
To the list of things that need not bother us.

But sometimes in our dreams we come to see
What it is we have but do not have—
A perfect friendship, an undying love
That all-triumphant will defy
Familiar failure; may for you
The dreamed-of prove quite possible,
May you wake, in time, into a morning world
Where that is so; that is my wish for you,
My dear, as you lay down to sleep,
And to the mercy of the night entrust yourself.

LOVE LOST

A proper winter reminds us of the attractions of months
When it never gets truly dark, when newspapers
Might be read outside at midnight, or close enough,
If only the news of the day by then were not so stale;
A cold blast from a thoroughly northern quarter
Brings nostalgia for better-behaved winds from the
    south,
Winds which at the end of their journey
Still retain some memory of those regions
Where it is not quite so important
That windows should close to with a tight fit.

What we do not have, we remember we once had;
Innocence glimpsed in others reminds us
Of the time when our own consciences were clear;
Birdsong heard on a still morning
Brings to mind the memory
That once the skies were filled with birds
And there were hedges and unruly places
For them to nest in; as the seas were full of fish
And there were fishermen with boats and songs
About fish and the catching of them.

What we lose, we think we lose forever,
But we are wrong about this; think of love—
When love is lost, we think it gone,
But it returns, often when least expected,
Forgives us our lack of attention, our failure of faith,

Our cold indifference; forgives us all this, and more;
Returns and says, "I was always there."
Love, *agape*, whispers, "Merely remember me,
Don't think I've gone away forever:
I am still here. With you. My power undimmed.
I never left you. See: I am here."

ON LOOKING AT A CHILD

Even the hours, I know, can be for you
A terribly long time; days even more so;
A week may be a lifetime, a month an era;
I would willingly exchange with you
My adult sense of subjective time
For yours, that allows the opportunity
To inhabit the present without
Thinking about its impending end;
In childhood we're briefly immortal;
That is why we pine, or some of us do,
For those long days of doing nothing
We used to have, that now we miss.

Looking at you, of course, reminds me
Of miracles—those occurrences
We are no longer allowed to believe in
Without the risk of mockery;
Science has taught us otherwise,
Although Science is a less benign
Parent than we hoped she would be;
If we were able, we might now undo
More and more of what she's brought us:
Artificial intelligence that will rob us
Of the illusion that we're useful,
That will take from us the comfort
Of the mundane tasks by which we live;
Nuclear physics, too, might be pruned
Of those parts that make our world

So dependent on a few red buttons,
Controlled, perhaps, by those
Who may find self-control a challenge,
The uninventing of that, and of the plastic
That is choking all we find beautiful
About our world, that's a revisionism
We all might practise, but can't do so with conviction:
The ancient story-tellers were right about this,
About how escaped genies are exactly that—
Escaped, and in general unwilling to return
To any durance of which we can conceive;
The wise can never become once again
The uninformed; the adult cannot reclaim
The innocence of the child; nobody who offers Eden
Is worth listening to; we know a false story
The moment it is told, and won't be fooled,
Or so we like to tell ourselves; experience
May suggest otherwise, but not for long;
We tumble to lies we wanted to believe
Once doubt nudges at belief insistently enough.

So, talk of miracles is pointless,
If not discouraged, then mocked at least,
By our compulsory code of realism;
Yet, looking at you, the language of miracles
Seems exactly right; your tiny hands
Are so perfect, intricate instruments
Made for mending watches, typing,
Stitching rendered tissue, arranging
The material world in ways we call art;

Your head, so small, is nonetheless
The locus of a galaxy of cells
Into which ancient wisdom is already encoded;
That makes me think of miracles again,
Even after the old saints, to whom
Miraculous power was attributed,
Have shuffled off, or been found
To be apocryphal; you, in spite of that
Are miraculous in my eyes,
As is love of others and its concomitant, kindness;
May the impulses that sustain all those
Still somehow function in a world
With no official role for miracles,
Other than as instances of things
We shouldn't believe in;
Allow us to negotiate and survive
The sterile corridors we've invented for ourselves,
And be in view once more, warm to the touch,
Beacons of light, reminders
Of a preciousness we might otherwise forget.

Of Books & Reading

THE GOODNESS OF BOOKS

I. THE BOOK BECOMES

On those sun-revealed classical shores,
Where, an age ago, the long memories
Of poets recorded the exploits
Of an obsessive hero and his men
Returning by perilous seas
To a home they had never quite forgotten,
There was no call for writing;
The reciter remembered, drew each detail
From a deep well of memory
That people had the time for then,
Before the invention of those things
That fill our lives today,
And stop the learning of poetry.

Later on, the scroll and wax tablet
Took the place of human recollection,
And laid the ground for the book,
That clever idea of stitching
Vellum together to make something
You could chain to a lectern
And read aloud from, with authority.
From that point, the book,
Unlike most inventions, became smaller,
Tentatively entered the individual home
And said, "Now, look at me,
And let me in, I have come to stay."

II. MOVEABLE TYPE

Happy that invention: now the least of men
Might participate in the secrets
The powerful kept to themselves;
A pauper may know what it is
To be a potentate; the most miserable
In durance vile may sense that freedom
Denied them in their world of confinement;
The victims of injustice, always there,
Might read of Justice and her triumphs,
And hope she'll notice them, and hear them too;
The hungry may read of plenty,
Those without love in their lives
May read about what it is
To be loved by another, and hope;
Books do all of this—and more.

III. WHAT THE BOOK IS

The book is a friend of truth—
Almost always; every so often
A misdirected intelligence
Gets it wrong and writes
A perfect shocker,
Some work of prose
That, with perverted poetry,
Inspires its readers to do evil;
There have been a few such books,
Each a monument, in its way,
To human malevolence,
But these are exceptions:
Books that do the opposite,
That cheer and inspire,
That persuade the rejected
That they will get a hearing;
These books make all the difference
To an out-of-kilter world,
Bring joy, bring understanding,
Are closed at the final page
And then kissed gently,
As one kisses something loved and cherished—
A lover's handkerchief,
A photograph of mother or of a spouse;
Such books remain with us for life,
Wise and unchanging,
Source of what we want so very much
To believe in and to preserve.

IV. ON THE BEDSIDE TABLE

Pray that in our later years
On our bedside table there will be
More books than jars of pills;

Pray that when we dim the light
It is on a world of complex plots
Rather than one of rancour;

Pray that we will still believe
It important that the heroine
Should still marry the hero;

Pray that to our children
We shall still give those books
We ourselves loved when young;

That the dish should still
Run away with the spoon
In an unwise elopement;

That the velveteen rabbit
Will never be made less tragic
By prescription antibiotics;

That pirates will still walk the plank
Rather than be given
The benefit of the doubt;

That at the end of the day
Scout and Jem will still
Be read to by Atticus Finch;

That mice and men
And great white whales
Will frolic in their elements;

Pray for all of that,
And for that device, the book,
Our beloved companion and our friend.

REMEMBERING MURIEL SPARK
a poem for a centenary

I.

As anniversaries go, twenty years
Allows for modest satisfaction:
So many of us manage two decades
That they usually pass unnoticed,
Unremarked upon by all
But our closest friends, and those
Who are prepared to forgive us
Most things, if not everything.

Fifty years is occasion, though,
For respectful re-assessment—
Out of the territory of base metal
Fifty basks, puts up feet
And enjoys the sun,
Does nothing, looks good,
Glances back a bit, smiles, remembers.

One hundred, though: centennial
Celebration, centennial cherishing
Is the key in which the conversation
Proceeds. Achieving the century
Puts one in a special category
Whether one is a cricketer,
A novelist, or just a person—
That last status being so undemanding
But ultimately all that matters.

II.

You saw so much; you saw the things
We knew were there but could
Not quite locate nor put in words
As good, as expertly wrought as yours.
You tripped us up when we, the unprepared,
Were not being careful enough,
You laid out unexpected things,
Remarks revealing sentiments
Other than those we expected,
Or matters made more complicated
By the intrusion of human deviousness
Or delicious human unpredictability.
Hah! we said; and then *Hah!* again.

III.

What was your parish?
Where the centre of your universe?
Everywhere, really, but at heart
And always, you were a citizen of Edinburgh;
Not just an inhabitant, but a citizen—
And there is a difference.

This city imbued you with its essence,
Its spikiness—look at its architecture
All stone and spikes, the soul
Of such a city is not a rounded,

Comfortable thing—it is sharp
And ready to see the spiky side of things.
You embodied that so effortlessly;
The characters you created
May have lived in many different places
But they all had Edinburgh
As their beginning, their nascence.

IV.

You will never leave us now;
Every so often, on a street,
We catch the Morningside tone,
Half forgotten, but still there,
Vaguely disapproving in its
Elongated vowels, some remark
That puts twenty-first century
Anodyne, undifferentiated Scotland
In its place. You did that so well,
Mutatis mutandis, in the temporal sense,
As you would undoubtedly say.

Those of slender means, those
Innocent schoolgirls made of yearning
And misinformation, those strange
Inhabitants of London's odd geography,
Swearing nuns, the blatantly manipulative,
The left-behind, the searchers—

Your parish was a broad one,
But home, here, this city
Claims you as its own,
Its beloved daughter, its sparkling Muse,
Embraces you in gratitude, remembers you.

GRAHAM GREENE

His novels show a good eye for dereliction:
A run-down hotel, a hinterland
Of unwelcoming hills; a jetty
In need of repair; a scruffy town bereft
Of diversion beyond the back-biting
Of stranded officials dependent
On the deceptive consolations of alcohol;
It was in these settings
That his imagination did its work.

He found them easily enough
With his novelist's nose for poverty
And a particular breed of loneliness;
Such things, after all,
Have a distinctive smell
And beckon with insistence
From behind the green baize door,
That conceals small secrets;
From the edge of the dusty road
That goes nowhere in particular;
From territories where wars have been,
Or are about to start;
And when it came to the *dramatis personae*,
A small cast was quite enough for him;
Not much beyond a priest

In whom faith has long since
Lost its battle, and who has given up
All thoughts of escape,
Having sensed, correctly,
That there is none; or a bureaucrat
Passed over for promotion once too often,
For whom the opportunities of adultery
Are the only small excitement;
Or those simply performing, with resignation,
The deadly jobs they've done for years.

Over such lives he cast
His feeling eye, recording
The particular shipwrecks
Of a ruined career, of small betrayals,
Of all those grubby features
That make of failure and seediness
Such absorbing reading; that was his land,
The terroir that made his vintage
So characteristically enticing;
Appreciative critics gave his name to it,
Eponymy being a distinction
To which few writers can aspire—
Greeneland, with a colonial architecture
All of its own, and a climate
That somehow suited the people
Sentenced to live there,
Who would wish to be somewhere else
But are too defeated to move.

They still exist, those places,
Although they have been cleaned up now,
Made safer and more accessible;
Improved by the bright lies
Of their meretricious salesmen;
A light has been shone into them
And this light fades the black and white
Of the picture he painted, turns it sepia,
Which is his colour, which is his mood.

A MAKER OF BEAUTIFUL BOOKS

A maker of beautiful books
Knows exactly what it is that makes
Paper, card, printer's ink,
The raw words of the writer
Into that lovely object
We call a book; understands
The subtle work of fonts,
Of leading, of bindings,
That makes a book something
We wish to hold to ourselves,
To keep and cherish, to read
At times when the soul is in need
Of solace, of insight, and art
That can transform the quotidian
Into the transcendent.

A maker of beautiful books
Understands that text
Should whisper to us its message
Like a confiding friend,
Not in the trumpet tones
Of the strident, the polemical,
But gently, tactfully,
In private places of exchange
Where the loud and the angry
Have no wish to linger.

A maker of beautiful books
Brings people together
In civil and gracious converse,
Helps the puzzled and confused
To understand what it is
That puzzles or confuses them;
Puts an end to that ignorance
On which evil parasitically
Thrives; shows the weak
The way to strength, brings
Freedom to the most remote corners,
Reminds us of love
And its manifold works.

A few years ago I was invited to speak at the Library of Congress in Washington. The entrance hall to the Library is famous for its murals, which present an unambiguous message to any politician who wanders in from Congress over the lawn. On the day that I visited, there was a memorial service taking place in the Congress buildings for a well-known African American politician. A line of mourners made their way in to pay their respects. There is always something particularly moving about people lined up to say goodbye in this way. In this case, I read in the papers that the politician in question had been the victim of disparagement. His response to this had been extremely dignified—always the best response to hurtful words.

LIBRARY OF CONGRESS

The frescoes here proclaim
Good government and the truth,
And the dangers of those things
That impede the proper living
Of the democratic life;
Anarchy sits with broken wheels,
Hewn building stones upended;
Idle youths and their corrupters
Occupy benches from which
Sorrowing industry and learning
Have been told to go;
There is no ambiguity here:
The visitor is cautioned and is left
In no doubt about what libraries,
And this particular one indeed

Mean; the message is spelled out
In words as well; there is no excuse
For missing it, and should you
Drop your eyes to the floor
And keep them low, it is inscribed
There as well, in marble and in brass.
Knowledge and the word
Are our foundation, and our sword.

Every day, twelve thousand items
Are received, and listed,
Filed away in boxes, put in store,
While librarians in droves
Prepare the patient shelves for more.
Knowledge and the word
Are our foundation, and our sword.

From the window at the front
Around the Congress building
Can be seen a line of mourners;
They shuffle forward, as those
Who pay respects to fallen heroes
Always shuffle, in silence;
A much-loved black congressman,
With a deep voice and a parish
Of suffering lies in state;
He endured the insults
Of an unkind opponent,
But answered to these slights:
Come down and see me, come
And see us, see how people live.

Places

GREECE

THE ORACLE AT DELPHI

Ill-tempered he may have been,
Adept at frightening too,
Zeus had form in this regard,
Transformed himself to snatch
Young Ganymede the shepherd
From his innocent pasture;
He could get away with that
Because he was Zeus after all
And gods are not subject to
The rules that make bourgeois life
So lacking in salience.

He found a much better use
For eagles, sent one from east
And one from west, they flew high
Until at length their dizzy flight
Converged; that marked the centre
Of the world, its true navel,
And the people placed a stone
On that exact spot, high above
The plains below Parnassus;
This was Delphi, a city
To which the known world then came,
To marvel at the temple
Where Apollo was worshipped,
To ask questions that could not

Be answered, other than in
Hexameters that none could
Make much sense of, which kept
The oracle's reputation
In high regard—a reply
That answers nothing will do
If you do not really
Want to know what the future
Holds, but feel you have to ask.

The passive tourists wander
Past the fallen stones and think
What they'd ask the oracle:
Does he love me as I love him?
Will she consent to be my wife?
Will I ever get the job
I've always wanted, and will
My name be up in lights?
Is it better to be poor
And contented, or be rich
And surrounded by flatterers
Who love you for what you've got?
Big questions, to which the reply
Is *Possibly, or maybe not,*
But in the meantime make the most
Of what you don't know, the wise
Do not always say what they know,
Remember that, forget the rest.

GOODBYE TO THE IONIAN

The latitudes from which we, pale sailors,
Accustomed to altogether colder waters
And insistent rain, are drawn,
Are northern ones; the voice
We hear in the wind says *north*;
Our hills whisper the same word;
North is their message, northern their faith,
And if, as is perhaps understandable,
We head south, only too ready
To believe that claims of a gentler Nature,
One receptive to olive trees and seas
That have too little room to be
Truly angry, then that is because
We hear another part of our psyche,
One that North herself has scolded
For being altogether unsuited
To a landscape of hills and mists
Appropriate to hills; of hills
That know what lies in store for them
As early as September these days,
When summer makes its excuses
For its behaviour, and leaves us to it.

Not imagining that we could ever
Fit as naturally into this world
As do the easy-living residents,
Who may have forgotten their classical heritage,
But who are proud enough of it anyway,

We nonetheless try to recall
Those bits that remain—the odd phrase,
The occasional memory of gods
And who they were, although it is
Only too easy to get them mixed up
And attribute to one a temper tantrum
Or a sulk that belonged to another.

Others have done the same,
Succumbed to the temptations
Of a beckoning South,
Famously so, in some cases,
Adopting a cause or subscribing
To a mood, a way of being,
As the romantic poets did;
Keats answered the call
Of shores very similar to these;
He was not the last poet
To make the understandable mistake,
Of getting too close
To a particular sort of beauty;
We're wiser now: we understand
That mists, though charming,
May at the same time be miasmic.

Of course, those who go elsewhere
Have to return; home awaits,
And smiles at the old story
That South presented,
Says: these things are illusions,

But nevertheless do the trick, enable you
To survive a winter, ignore
The things you'd like to ignore,
By simply closing your eyes and
Seeing Ithaca again, and its sea,
And a shore of rounded stones,
Blue and white, washed smooth,
On which Odysseus himself
Set foot in coming home.

SCOTLAND

ST. KILDA

I.

Sometimes things are firmly settled;
Sometimes a slow decline of population
Becomes a demographic rout,
And none are left, as when in dark times
Some remote village falls to an invader
And suddenly everyone is no more;
The houses are forlorn and empty,
The animals stand in their fields
Confused at the end of human order,
The crops are ungathered,
The fruit falls unappreciated from the trees,
Weeds claim the beds and barrows.
The things we do, or do not do
In one place are felt not only there
But elsewhere; what happens
At one time happens at other times too;
No one thing is beyond the influence of other things:
Small islands share the sea with large islands,
Share the clouds that sweep their mutual sky,
Share the rain and wind, unpredicted gales,
Share the songs and the things
That brought forth the songs.

Here the boats arrived, on time,
To take those things away.

II.

Here, on this lonely rock, gannets
Countless in their multitude
Lay claim to a home, the circling seas
A reminder of the smallness
Of the land and of our lives.

The slopes are almost white with birds,
Nesting, arguing, caught in flight,
Swooping down ravines that end
In a churning sea.

These cliffs are on the edge of a great emptiness
Of water and sky, but the rocks themselves
Are all claimed by a noisy tenantry
Keen to attract or to repel,
Using different vocables for each.
Replete with fish they housekeep
Their nests, their perches giddy
Above a restless sea.

Flight is a constant
Obligation of birds,
Depends on the flow of air
And the winds that bring the air
From somewhere that is not here,
And will not remain for long;
So we, and the birds about us,
Are partners in impermanence.

To glide above the sea
On currents of moving air,
The wind, requires tiny
Adjustments of wings,
And a sense of height, born
Of having been raised
On the edge of a void,
Until suddenly, one day,
You launch yourself,
Become a bird.

Birds, we are told, create invisible boundaries,
Across water and land, mark out
Territory we cannot see;
They choose to be with others
Who see the world from the same angle
As they do, share habits;
So the skies here may at times
Be black with puffins,
Or white with gannets,
Obeying some ancient
Division decreed by deviation
From a common ancestor.

Gannets climb, sharp-eyed,
From airy heights they
See into the water below,
Watch the movement of fish,
Drop like stones,
Fall into the water
With the same splash

That Icarus made;
Unlike him, they surface.

The life of birds responds
To currents we do not see;
Birds must follow
Precepts decreed
A long time ago,
And immutable;
They have enviable freedom—
Air is unconstraining—
But biology holds them
To a life of fish and squabble.

III.

And the sheep, too, were a necessary
Part of this life; they led their lives
Unaware of loneliness, unaware
Even of Lewis and the Uists
Across those miles of sea:

Now they cling to the impossible slopes,
Leading an angled life
That is nothing to do with
Any human husbandry;
Their owners left many years ago,
A full life-span ago, and more;
They remain, survive the gales,
To meet what few sheep meet:
A death from old age.

IV.

"Isolation," you say, "is a condition
That reminds us of its own name,
And the roots of that name—*isola*, an island;
To be isolated is to be apart from those
Who are otherwise close to you,
But who, when they look towards you,
See only water, as you see water
When you look towards them;
Isolation, though, enables the ear to hear
Those sounds that are often drowned out:
The sound of the heart, the sound of the blood
In the veins; the sound of the wind's breathing,
The sound of still water, unsuspected of movement,
The sound of love and affirmation."

V.

From the hills of Lewis
Hazy on the horizon an island
May be spotted; blue, washed
Like a watercolour, fading,
Reappearing briefly, and then
Gone once more, like signals
From the ether, faint messages
From afar, lost in static,
Barely received, only half understood:
People lived here once . . . Their life was birds
And the eggs of the birds they hunted . . .

In the winter months, short days
Of gales . . . but in summer, the nights
That were almost days . . . Remember
Us and the place in which we lived,
Our names, the way we looked,
The words and sounds we left behind.

Scotland is a small country, and yet it is the smallness of Scotland that gives it the character that claims the hearts of so many. This poem is about smallness, and the importance of the local. It is about Scotland, but it could be about anywhere local—anywhere that is important to people because it is their place.

DEAR ONE

Dear one, how many years is it—I forget—
Since that luminous evening when you joined us
In the celebration of whatever it was that we were
    celebrating—I forget—
It is a mark of a successful celebration
That one should have little recollection of the cause;
As long as happiness itself remains a memory.
Our tiny planet, viewed from afar, is a place of swirling
    clouds
And dimmish blue; Scotland, though lodged large in all
    our hearts,
Is invisible at that distance, not much perhaps,
But to us it is our all, our place, the opposite of nowhere;
Nowhere can be seen by looking up
And realising, with shock, that we really are very small;
You would say, yes, we are, but never overcompensate,
Be content with small places, the local, the short story
Rather than the saga; take pleasure in private jokes,
In expressions that cannot be translated,
In references that can be understood by only two
    or three,

But which speak with such eloquence for small places
And the fellowship of those whom you know so well
And whose sayings and moods are as familiar
As the weather; these mean everything,
They mean the world, they mean the world.

Angus Lordie, one of the characters in the *Scotland Street* novels, is given to reflecting on how he feels about Scotland. Here he is, at a lunch in the Tuscan countryside, remembering where he comes from and what that means.

SCOTLAND'S CLAIM

Dear friends, there is no timetable
For happiness; it moves, I think, according
To rules of its own. When I was a boy
I thought I'd be happy tomorrow;
As a young man I thought it would be
Next week; last month I thought
It would be never. Today, I know
It is now. Each of us, I suppose,
At least one person who thinks
That our manifest faults are worth ignoring;
I have found mine, and am content.

When we are far from home
We think of home; I, who am happy today,
Think of those in Scotland for whom
Such happiness might seem elusive;
May such powers as listen to what is said
By people like me, in olive groves like this,
Grant to those who want friendship a friend,
Attend the needs of those who have little,

Hold the hand of those who are lonely,
Allow Scotland, our place, our country,
To sing in the language of her choosing
That song she's always wanted to sing,
Which is of brotherhood, which is of love.

Cities are about friendship. They are about intricate and elaborate networks of friendship. Here is Angus Lordie, addressing his friends at a party in Scotland Street, at the end of one of the novels, when he feels he has to say something about how he feels about Edinburgh.

EDINBURGH

Dear friends, we are the inhabitants
Of a city which can be loved, as any place may be,
In so many different and particular ways;
But who amongst us can predict
For which reasons, and along which fault lines,
Will the heart of each of us
Be broken? I cannot, for I am moved
By so many different and unexpected things: by our sky,
Which at each moment may change its mood at whim
With clouds in such a hurry to be somewhere else;
By our lingering haars, by our eccentric skyline,
All crags and spires and angular promises,
By the way we feel in Scotland, yes, simply that;
These are things that break my heart
In a way for which I am never quite prepared—
The surprises of a love affair that lasts a lifetime.
But what breaks the heart the most, I think,
Is the knowledge that what we have
We all must lose; I don't much care for denial,
But if pressed to say goodbye, that final word

On which even the strongest can stumble,
I am not above pretending
That the party continues elsewhere,
With a guest list that's mostly the same,
And every bit as satisfactory;
That what we think are ends are really adjournments,
An *entr'acte*, an interval, not real goodbyes;
And perhaps they are, dear friends, perhaps they are.

A FRAGILE BEAUTY

This city woos you gently
As a tactful lover does,
One who says, yes, I am listening,
But do not overwhelm me
With excessive praise;
Do not expect me to respond
To ebullient adjectives;
Over-statement will get you nowhere
In a subtle love affair.

Rather, this city promises
Gentle heartbreak, you will not find
In this city's repertoire,
The grand architectural gesture,
Echoing squares, statements
Of imperial ambition;
But you will find harmony,
You will find the quiet
Resolved beauty of streets
That go somewhere with modesty,
Not in too great a rush
To get to their destination;
You will find skies that transform
Themselves hourly, if not by the minute,
As if changing, deliberately,
The circumstances of an assignation.

This city is a reserved lover,
The greys of its time-darkened stone
Are attenuated by reticence;
It has a quiet and fragile beauty:
There are other places
That can shout, this city whispers.

And its words are brief
And may be missed at times
By those not paying attention;
It says: look, I am here,
I am yours; for your love,
And in exchange, my beauty
I give to you, I give to you.

THE SEVEN HILLS OF EDINBURGH

THE CASTLE ROCK

(The Castle Rock dominates Edinburgh. For
invaders it has been an obvious prize. Prince Charles
Edward Stuart attempted to take it, but the garrison
held out, and he went on elsewhere.)

If there is one thing that appeals
To those who would exercise dominion,
It is a high vantage point, a rock
That commands the land about it;
Were you, in that distant twelfth century,
To be seeking somewhere secure,
Your eye might fall, not accidentally,
On this particular salience,
With its steep sides, its cliffs,
Up which only the most determined raiders
Would think of climbing,
And then only those, a minority I'm sure,
Who are indifferent to the discouragement
A defender might send cascading down;
Gardy-loo was rarely cried
By those who poured burning oil
On unwelcome visitors.

History here has an uncomfortable face,
A consequence of intrigues hatched

By Scotland's incorrigible plotters;
It would be comforting to conclude
That Scotland became less violent,
That people saw the repetitive error
Of their combative ways;
They did not: power, in our latitudes,
Has always been a matter of bettering others
And then celebrating that victory
With banishment of the defeated, and worse.
All of that is here in these stones,
And, of course, a prominence like this
Attracts those who wish to stand on rocks
And crow; how tempting, then, it was
For that ambitious young man from France,
A pretender's sprig, bedecked in tartan,
To blockade this rock, though never win it,
Even as he claimed a kingdom he had never seen
With the assistance of those he had never met.

From the ramparts of the castle that bestrides it
A daily shot is fired, a way of punctuating time;
Down below, those who live in this place
Look briefly up, remembering where they are,
Of what town they are citizens,
And are reminded, too, of what particular rock
Watches over them. Satisfied that it is one o'clock,
Absorbed in its quotidian tasks,
Edinburgh drifts into afternoon,
Beneath a rock that is both hill and metaphor.

CRAIGLOCKHART HILL,
A CENTURY AGO

(It was on Craiglockhart Hill that the Craiglockhart
War Hospital for Officers treated many victims of
shell shock and other injuries, including the poets
Wilfred Owen and Siegfried Sassoon.)

There are two hills here under the umbrella
Of a single name; sometimes a hill conceals
Another hill behind it, the real goal;
Hill-walkers complain of that illusion,
Believing they have reached the summit,
They discover it lies onc layer beyond
The high ground they have just reached:
A familiar issue for most of us,
Even if our ambitions are more modest
Than those of sturdy Munro-baggers.

Craiglockhart Hill, like many a Scottish hill,
Has seen a private slice of history
Striated with pain; a century ago,
Young men wounded in body and spirit
Spent long months on the north face of this hill
Recovering from that great stramash of men
In broken, tortured Europe; they knew
The lie on all the public posters claimed,
The *dolce et decorum* call by those
Who never saw the trenches nor the blood
That broke men's hearts, and their bodies too;

This hill hosted their hospital, a retreat
For the soul-injured, quiet, far from the guns,
Open to the winds that blow across the Forth,
Bearing the scent of gorse, and that of sea,
A wind to dry their tears, make whole again
The shattered and the saddened;
In these northern nights might men sleep once more,
Free from torment, from the anger of the guns,
Far from collective madness; if refuge
Can bring healing, then it must show to us
The image of love, through quietus glimpsed.

ARTHUR'S SEAT AND GEOLOGY

(In 1788, James Hutton, the founder of modern
geology, published his "Theory of the Earth," a work
that unseated long-held religious notions of the
Earth's age.)

This is a crouching lion, watching,
As crouching lions will do, over
The territory of a circumscribed back yard;
This hill had the crusty lion-heart
Of a volcano, now no more,
It lives on memories of long-cooled
Fiery moments; it never vitrified
A city, as Vesuvius did; its belches
Frightened nobody, as there
Was nobody then to frighten;
Now we climb, innocent children,
On rocks that once glowed red,
Follow an easy route to the summit,
Close our eyes and feel the breeze
That whips round the Pentlands
Or goads us with its North Sea taunts.

Even in retirement, though,
The crags that frown on Holyrood,
Made something happen
When James Hutton looked at them, reached
A moment of understanding,
And realised the theology of creation

Was all wrong; the earth to Mr. Hutton
Seemed punished by its energy;
Twisted into shapes imposed by a molten
And unforgiving heart; here and there
In efforts of escape mountains shrugged off
The constraining mantle, displaying for us to see—
If only we would look—the history of all things
In lines of rock, layers of magma, fossils, littered
Paths of glaciers. How it humbled him
To read that past, and see how long it was.

IMAGINED CONVERSATION ON
BLACKFORD HILL

On Blackford Hill, my dear, where, in summer,
The fields, in their promised fullness of grass,
Are sweet upon the air, where a few miles off
The shy Pentlands suggest a hinterland
Of farms, of rivers, and of Border towns,
We rested on a half-completed walk;
You pointed to the Observatory nearby
And said, "What do you think they really see?"
I could have answered, "Everything, I think,"
For Blackford is the only Scottish hill
On which the ordinary course of work
Is to question how planets come to be,
About how worlds, and all that they contain—
Flowers and stock exchanges and waterfalls—
Developed as they did, routinely talk
Of an unseen world of particles, how they
Move and die, spark briefly, things beyond the grasp
Of two average walkers, unversed in physics,
For whom the journal *Nature* is too hard to comprehend.
You say, "Professor Higgs worked not far from here,
Barely half a mile away." I nod and say, "He did,"
And point out the path we must take to descend,
Drawn by gravity, another force we cannot see.

CORSTORPHINE HILL

(Corstorphine Hill is thought to have inspired
Kidnapped by Robert Louis Stevenson.)

Mull, Glencoe, Rannoch Moor
Were the earlier stages
Of a walk ending here
With a simple handshake,
As Alan Breck Stewart
Left David Balfour;
Stevenson is so real
We might almost believe
That it happened.

Corstorphine Hill surveys
A city rich in all
The things that he admired;
From his bed of sickness
Young RLS looked out,
Saw Leerie light his lamp,
Saw shadows in the night,
Dreamed of adventurous
Escape, of flight.

Drawn to this hill, he let
His imagination
People it with heroes,
Saw David Balfour off

On his perilous way,
Even now, so many
Years from that narrative,
The tree-girt hill invites
Shared mystery.

ON CALTON HILL

A hill, or any place of heights,
May both stand out and simply stand
For something quite beyond itself:
Everest stands for all the things
We can only do at the very limits
Of our ability; man can climb it,
But only just, and many find
The death zone means exactly what it says,
May find, too, that where oxygen is thin
People are slow to help one another.

Similarly, a mountain may stand for purity,
As does Mont Blanc, white-topped, unsullied,
Or, under its Aegean sky, Olympus
Stands for a whole theology of gods
Given to intemperate, selfish power
Exercised by those who like to hurl
Thunderbolts, to punish mortals
For being themselves, not gods,
And sometimes irritating, or scared.

Calton Hill, a moderate slope
By any standards, is inimical to gods,
Portrays the role of intellect; few hills
Give room to philosophers, as this hill does;
Few hills attempt to embody reason
As understood during that brief

Moment of clarity when Edinburgh
Put Enlightenment at its heart.
Order pervades the human contribution
To this hill's restrained appearance:
The buildings here are classical,
A Grecian dream realised in Scottish stone;
Here the measured life may confidently be led;
Reason and wisdom both thrive under the aegis
Of an architecture that embodies
An ancient ideal, sensitive to proportion.
Looking west from here, down bustling Princes Street,
We're reminded of all those truths
That Dugald Stewart, David Hume, and Adam Smith
All professed to us: be sympathetic,
For human sympathy is all; take note
Of the needs of others; avoid the dark;
Let justice prevail, and pay heed to light.

BRAID HILLS

In another culture, a place like this
With its commanding views
And its sufficient otherness
From the city down below,
Might be a site of pilgrimage,
A holy place, just far enough away
To be worth travelling to,
And quiet enough to permit
The occasional miracle; not here—
The deities worshipped on these hills
Are *bogies, birdies, eagles,*
And the greatest of them all, the *hole-in-one,*
Cause of generous libation
In the temples of tweed and spiked shoes
In which these pilgrims gather.

On Buckstone Snab a laid-out map
Will show you where others are,
The points by which we fix
Our position in this world.
Their names are lovely, might be sung:
Knock Wood, East Lomond, and Cat Law,
Other hills that are small and distant.
Whatever hill you're on, this says,
There will be another—a metaphor for life,
Perhaps, to keep us in our place,
Which now, at this moment,
Is on Buckstone Snab, with a wind
From the south west, with scurrying clouds.

Unrelated Poems

Here are three poems about Canada, a country in which I have spent some time and for which I have great admiration. The first is about the "northness" of Canada and how that contrasts with the passionate nature that we, who live in the north, imagine we see in warmer climes. Canada stands for courtesy, kindness, restraint—all the things we really need in a world of disharmony and strife.

NORTHLAND

North is a way of looking
At a world in which south
Is synonymous with an altogether
Different slant to the sun
And a mood music that
Observes an unrelated key;
There is no necessary connection
Between courtesy and latitude,
Although sometimes, as in this case,
It seems to occur—the compass
By which north is identified
Is in this case marked *kindness* and *modesty:*
Small words for a large country
And a whole way
Of looking at the world.

Some years ago I visited a friend who has a cottage in Eastern Ontario. One evening, my friend demonstrated to me an unexpected talent.

WOLVES

I read Farley Mowat and thought
I knew something about wolves,
About how they run down
Their prey in lengthy pursuit,
About the long brotherhoods
Of wolves and their lonely deaths;
I thought I knew about all that
Until I heard a wolf howl in the night,
And was unprepared
For what I heard, for the keening
Of it, the utter desolation.

We stood outside, my friend and I,
With the world white about us
As he cupped his hands
And howled into the darkness;
From somewhere far away
Came a response, a howl so sad
That no words could describe
The regret of it, the loneliness:
Yes, I am here, it must have said;
Yes, I am here, and that is all.

In Winnipeg a few years ago, on a cold fall day, I visited the remarkable Museum of Human Rights. Outside, on the pathway by which you approach the museum, is a statue of Gandhi.

THE CANADIAN MUSEUM FOR HUMAN RIGHTS IN WINNIPEG

A late fall day, I look up
At the large and beautiful museum—
Large, of necessity, because
The wrongs we do one another
Require a lot of space.
Before it, suddenly, a statue;
He is so small, this man
From another place, another age,
He walks purposefully, smiling;
Gandhi never said
Things would be perfect,
And they aren't, yet we
Remember him, as we do now,
And think, perhaps, how much worse
They could have been.
The door opens; I pass from the cold
Manitoba air into a place of warmth
And charity, of faith, a museum
That says: just stop and think:
So much in life is unavoidable,
But these things we'll show you here
Are clearly not—remember that.

This occurred to me in the lift of the Oberoi Trident Hotel in Mumbai. I was travelling to our rooms on the thirty-first floor, rooms from which we were afforded a fine view of the bay. This is the Arabian Sea. There were two mysterious floors above us, harbouring, I suspected, marbled rooms of unspeakable opulence. Who frequented those rooms, and how did they get there? The poem addresses the issue of desert and outcome in terms of the allocation of hotel rooms.

FROM A MUMBAI HOTEL

Obedient in all its essentials
The hotel lift climbs skywards;
We trust the engineering
That suspends us here:
Stairs are solid, can be seen,
Require no faith, but take
Time from those who believe
That time is what they do not have.

To the thirty-first of thirty-three
Floors I travel; right above
Are quarters of unfathomable luxury,
Where only those who have, with purpose,
Fashioned a life of comfort for themselves
Out of the lives of many others,
May look out from quadrilateral windows
On a city of this many souls;
Hotel rooms are not a matter of desert;
Do not make that fond mistake

Made by so many who believe in justice,
That you get in life the hotel room
You deserve; you do not:
Hotel rooms, as we come to learn,
Are allocated on Darwinian principles:
And not on the grounds that the best rooms
Go to the best—that simply is not true.

Hotel rooms say nothing of those
Who pitch their tent in them,
We leave nothing of ourselves behind
To say that we were there;
Chambermaids prepare our room
With quiet impartiality, keep to themselves
The secrets they unearth, or stumble upon;
Only the cost is counted, that alone
Is recorded on the bill, paid and forgotten,
Part of nobody's history of anything.

Once, at a meeting in New York,
I heard the question posed: *Where are they,*
These others? And answered thus: *I'll tell you:*
They are in a hotel room named failure.
Uncharitable, yes, but, in essence, true:
Our hotel rooms are named:
Do not think you can change the description
Of the hotel room you're given,
Rearrange the furniture,
Nor keep the world from intruding
When you display *Do not disturb*

Upon your door; you will be,
For Hubris may occupy
A high enough room, but
Nemesis is the one who operates the lift.

Outside the window is Mumbai,
Circling kites navigate the air
Above the great city spread below;
In the bay, a fisherman casts a net;
Crawling cars are sluggish blood
In the concrete arteries; life is difficult
For most, who must struggle
With this traffic and these distances,
With heat and dust and failed rains,
And the simple mathematics
Of the Malthusian nightmare,
Each in the metaphorical hotel room
Chance and a handful of decisions
Have brought him to; if there are gods
Listening in this city's temples,
Colourful actors in an ancient tale,
Look with generosity on these
Patient people, bring rain, prosperity,
Happiness—all the things they want,
Make peaceable their dreams.

FISH, AND THE THOUGHTS OF FISH

Underwater is different,
For the water divides light
In ways that fish understand
Instinctively, but at which
We, the land-bound ones,
Can only marvel wordlessly:
It is a blessing, perhaps,
That, clever as we are,
We have not yet learned
To talk underwater.

Fish have water as
Their firmament;
The stars for fish are
Distant and dangerous light,
Not somewhere
They would wish to look at,
Nor wish upon.

Fish have mountains,
As we have;
These are sunken rocks,
Around which
All but the smallest fish
May swim with ease;
For a fish to climb
A submarine mountain
Without water

Is as difficult as for a man
To climb Everest without oxygen.
It's the same thing,
Say fish; it's the same thing
But viewed from
A different perspective.

Love, say fish,
Is much the same thing as water;
Without it all about us,
We feel dry.

The penultimate poem in this collection was written after a friend and I dealt with a fallen young oak tree in Kirkcudbrightshire. The tree had blown over; we pulled it into the upright position and secured it with ropes. It is still standing.

SAVING AN OAK TREE

Even the strongest of trees, when young,
Are vulnerable to wind and rain;
Earth softens, a bolus of roots
May wrench itself free of the soil's embrace;
A tree may fall for many reasons,
Just as we may fall, in our individual ways.

Summer this year has been wet,
Something to do, we are told,
With a trapped jet stream
Above our corner of north-west Europe;
When we look at the sky
We cannot see the wind—
Only the things that wind does,
Just as we cannot see friendship
If we look into the heart of another,
But can feel its effect; just as we feel
The wind on our faces, or the sun.

Rescuing the oak, we pushed and shoved
And brought it to its feet again;
Ropes around its juvenile trunk

Secured with knots to neighbouring trees
Were like the bonds that unite
One to another, the tendons of community,
The bindings of brotherhood.
A tree may be tied in place
Upright against the wind
With cord that is the same as that which ties
Us to our place in the world,
That long ago secured our people
To the place they inhabited,
To that place they loved enough to name.

And lastly, a personal note on friends.

FRIENDSHIP

Sometimes I look at my life
And reflect, as I suspect we all do,
On what I have not done;
On the things that I thought
I might achieve, but never did;

When I was a boy
There were so many others
So very much better
Than I was at the things
That boys like to do;
I lived in fear that
The incipient mesomorphs
Would practice their
Martial arts on me;
I ran away from
The challenges of sports
That required the ability
I could admire in those
With sporting names
Like Eric and Joe,
And a good eye
For the rugby ball
And its eccentric trajectory.

Later, I discovered, there were
Plenty of others more adept
At being popular, with more
Invitations to parties
To which I would like
To be invited; I didn't know
That most of us feel that,
Though rarely say it.

Even now, when I have done
Things I never thought I'd do,
I still have a list
Of things unattained;
It's too late
To learn the piano,
Too late to drive
A car capable of sixty
Up a hill, or indulge
In a Morgan three-wheeler;
I'd catch cold in a car
With no roof,
And possibly die.

But then I think
Of one thing I have
That means a hundred times
All this; I think of my friends,

And marvel at the good fortune
I have in them; for I have
Friends few, it seems,
Might ever find, and the gold
Of their nature lines my safe.